The Hockey Book for Girls

Written by
Stacy Wilson

Kids Can Press

With love to my heroes — my mom and dad

Acknowledgments

Thanks to my editor Liz MacLeod for her professional and gentle guidance; Karen Powers for her involving design; Kids Can Press for believing in the project; Karyn Bye and Shannon Miller for taking time out of their busy schedules to answer my questions; my first hockey coach, Bud Tait, who gave me the chance to play at a time when many coaches would have said, "Girls can't play hockey"; the Salisbury and Petitcodiac Minor Hockey Association; the Canadian Hockey Association; Maritime Sports and the Blades; and the New Brunswick Hockey Association. Special thanks to Jo and Misch for sharing in the victories and defeats. Thank you to my brother Shane for never getting tired of playing "Five Goals Goes in Net" and my sister Shelley for the "Letting Go."

Text copyright © 2000 by Stacy Wilson
Illustrations copyright © 2000 by Bill Slavin

Kids Can Press acknowledges the financial support of the Ontario Arts Council, the Canada Council for the Arts and the Government of Canada, through the BPIDP, for our publishing activity.

Published in Canada by
Kids Can Press Ltd.
29 Birch Avenue
Toronto, ON M4V 1E2

Published in the U.S. by
Kids Can Press Ltd.
4500 Witmer Estates
Niagara Falls, NY 14305-1386

Kids Can Press is a Nelvana company

Edited by Elizabeth MacLeod
Designed by Karen Powers
Printed in Hong Kong by Wing King Tong Company Limited

CM 00 0 9 8 7 6 5 4 3 2 1
CM PA 00 0 9 8 7 6 5 4 3 2 1

Canadian Cataloguing in Publication Data

Wilson, Stacy
  The hockey book for girls

Includes index.

ISBN 1-55074-860-2 (bound)   ISBN 1-55074-719-3 (pbk.)

1. Hockey for girls — Juvenile literature. I. Title.

GV848.6.W6W54 2000   j796.962'083'42   C99-932907-3

Photo Credits

Frank Baldassarra: front cover, 1, back cover.
Bruce Bennett Studios: 4 (left), 5 (bottom right), 7 (middle), 28, 31 (bottom), 33 (top right), 35 (both), 36 (left, top right).
Karyn Bye Collection: 34 (all).
Canadian Hockey Association Collection: 33 (bottom left and right).
Canadian Sport Images: 4 (bottom right), 5 (left), 23 (left), 7 (left), 31 (top), 36 (bottom right), 37 (both), 38 (left), 39 (top).
City of Toronto Archives: 5 (top right).
Brett Groehler Photography: 13 (bottom left), 29 (right), 39 (bottom left).
Paul Lynch Photography: 30 (bottom).
Ken Moran Photography: 29 (left).
Carole Morissette Photography: 8 (left).
Dale Preston Photography: 10, 11 (bottom left), 13 (top left), 14 (top left), 15 (bottom), 16 (all), 17 (right), 18 (both), 19 (top, bottom left), 27 (bottom left), 30 (top), 38 (right).
R&G Photo, Calgary: 7 (bottom), 9 (top).
Ron Ward Photography: 6 (all), 7 (top), 8 (right), 9 (middle), 11 (top, right), 12 (both), 14 (bottom left, right), 15 (top), 17 (left), 19 (bottom right), 20 (both), 21 (top and bottom left), 22 (all), 23 (right), 24 (both), 25 (left), 26, 27 (top left, top and bottom right).
Stacy Wilson Collection: 4 (top right), 13 (right), 25 (right), 32 (all), 33 (top left), 39 (bottom left).
USA Hockey: 21 (right).

Contents

Olympic Glory

Butterflies danced in my stomach as I lined up to take the opening face-off of the first Olympic hockey game played by Canadian women. Canada won the game, and I scored once and got two assists.

Canada, China, Finland, Japan, Sweden and the United States battled for top spot. On February 17, 1998, the first Olympic gold medal for women's hockey was placed around the neck of Cammi Granato, the U.S. captain. Canada won silver and Finland took bronze. Women's hockey had finally made it to the Olympics!

▲ Stacy at age eight.

Early days

Captaining the Canadian women's hockey team at the 1998 Olympics in Nagano, Japan, was a long way from the outdoor rink in Salisbury, New Brunswick, where I started playing hockey. I was eight years old, wore snowmobile mitts for hockey gloves and played on a boys' team.

A great moment

March 25, 1990, Ottawa, Ontario: The noise was deafening as 9000 fans screamed with excitement. Team Canada had just made history by winning the first International Ice Hockey Federation Women's World Championships.

▲ At the 1998 Olympics, captain Cammi Granato led her team to a gold medal.

▶ Kim Ratushny, Dawn McGuire and France St. Louis (left to right) after winning the 1990 World Championships.

Overtime heroics

The score was 3–3 after three periods at the 1997 Women's World Hockey Championships. For the first time in World Championship play, a game was going into overtime. The U.S. team was trying to win its first World Championships, while Canada was going for its fourth straight gold medal.

At 12:59 into overtime, Nancy Drolet of Canada completed her hat trick. Canada was still undefeated in World Championship play since it began in 1990. What a winning streak! You can see in the photo below how happy I was to captain such a great team.

▲ Did you know that women have been playing hockey for over 100 years? Women played hockey as early as the late 1800s. They wore long skirts, which they sometimes cleverly used to hide the puck from their opposition.

Fans, fans, fans

On January 16, 1998, a crowd of 14 944 fans filed into GM Place in Vancouver, British Columbia, to watch Canada play the United States (right). This was the largest audience to ever come out to watch a women's hockey game. The atmosphere was electric as Canada won 2–1. But the U.S. team turned it around on January 26, winning 3–1 in front of an even larger crowd of 15 163 fans at the Saddledome in Calgary, Alberta.

What Position Do You Want to Play?

▼ Picture yourself in goalie gear as a player races toward you. She unleashes a wrist shot and the puck flies. You catch it — what a great glove save! You are your team's last line of defense.

▼ Now see yourself as a forward sprinting down the ice, passing the puck to your linemate, then driving to the net. She fires a hard, low shot that bounces off the goalie's pads. You quickly slap the rebound into the net past the goaltender. Goal!

▼ Or pretend you're playing defense as an opposing forward skates toward you with the puck. You control the space between the two of you and keep yourself between her and your net. Now use your stick to knock the puck off her stick. One of your teammates grabs the puck. You've just prevented a scoring chance and given the puck back to your team.

Which position sounds fun to you? There are six hockey players per team on the ice at a time: one goaltender, two defense players (called a pair, or partners), and three forwards (called a line: left wing, center and right wing).

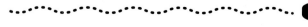

What else do you do when you're playing hockey?

▶ Goalies sometimes dash out of the crease to stop the puck behind the net. You leave the puck there for your defense or pass it.

◀ If you're on defense, you must quickly move the puck up ice, but still be able to return to defensive positioning quickly if your team loses the puck.

▶ Forwards must also play defensive hockey. Be ready to skate back into your defensive zone and cover an opponent so she doesn't get a chance to make a play or score. Centers have the added responsibility of taking the face-off, or draw. As soon as the official drops the puck, try to move it to a teammate using your stick or skates.

→ Try It!

Did you picture yourself in each of those hockey positions? If you did, you're using a skill that every top hockey player uses. It's called visualization. That means picturing a scene in your mind exactly the way that you want it to happen.

Visualizing lets you practice skills in any situation. I often pictured myself playing in overtime of a gold-medal World Championship game. When I was in exactly that situation in 1997, I had already gone through it in my mind so many times that I felt confident.

How do you visualize? Start by picturing simple skills a few times a week for five to ten minutes. Then progress to tougher skills and team plays. Always see yourself performing the skill correctly and successfully. For example, forwards could visualize receiving a pass and scoring.

Who Rules?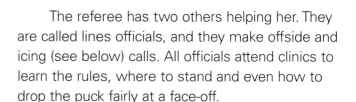

The whistle blows, and everyone on and off the ice stops to look at the woman wearing the black-and-white-striped sweater. She signals a penalty with her hands and calls out, "Number Eight red, two minutes for slashing."

That woman in stripes is the referee and she's in charge, making sure both teams play fair. She calls penalties on players who break the rules.

The referee must be in good physical condition because she skates for the whole game without a chance to change lines the way you and I do. As captain, I sometimes talked with refs about calls that my coach didn't agree with or a ruling that wasn't clear. I made sure I showed respect by speaking to her calmly, not angrily, and asking her to explain the rule or what she saw.

The referee has two others helping her. They are called lines officials, and they make offside and icing (see below) calls. All officials attend clinics to learn the rules, where to stand and even how to drop the puck fairly at a face-off.

Here are a few of the rules you need to know.

▼ Offside

You're offside if you cross your opponent's blue line (see the rink diagram on the next page) before the puck. However, the lines official won't blow her whistle until you or a teammate touch the puck in your opponent's zone. If you skate out of the zone before this happens, you won't be offside. You can now re-enter the offensive zone without an offside call. When an offside is called, a face-off takes place at one of the face-off dots just outside the blue line.

Icing

You'll be called for icing if you shoot the puck from your own side of center ice past your opponent's goal line without anyone touching it. Then the puck is dropped in a face-off in one of the circles next to your net. You are not called for icing if your team is short-handed, or one of the other team's players (except the goalie) could have touched the puck before it crossed the goal line but chose not to, or if you score.

Penalty

If you trip, hook, hold or elbow another player, etc., you'll be given a minor penalty. You must sit in the penalty box for two minutes while your team plays shorthanded. That means that your team has to play with one less player for two minutes or until your opponents score a goal, whichever comes first.

If you high stick, slash really hard or attempt to injure another player, you may be given a major penalty. You'll sit out for at least five minutes no matter how many goals the other team scores.

As you can see, when you get a penalty you are putting your team at a disadvantage. So ask your coach about any rules you don't understand. Rules are a part of all sports. They are what make games challenging and fun to play.

Any hockey player can trip another player and take the puck. It takes real skill and determination to get the puck fairly. So show respect for this exciting game and those who play it by playing within the rules. You'll feel good about your play and yourself.

▲ Lines officials watch that teams don't have too many players on the ice.

◀ Tripping lands you in the penalty box for two minutes and puts your team at a disadvantage.

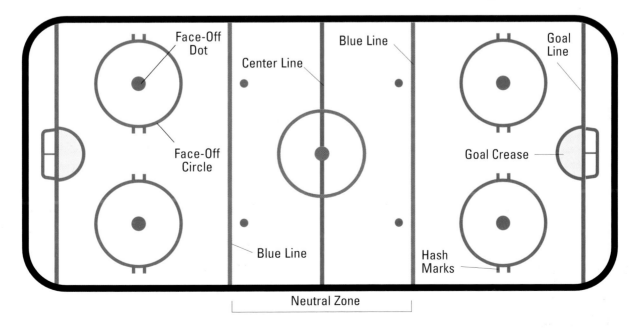

Face-Off Dot

Blue Line

Goal Line

Center Line

Face-Off Circle

Goal Crease

Blue Line

Hash Marks

Neutral Zone

Wear the Right Stuff

Hockey is an exciting game played at top speed. To make the sport as safe as possible, you need to wear protective hockey equipment. It doesn't matter if it's new or used as long as it protects you, fits properly and feels comfortable.

Shoulder pads ▶

Padding should wrap around the sides of your chest and just touch your pants in the back. The arm padding should be hard and overlap the elbow pads, and the shoulder caps should fit right on the shoulder. To protect your back, get shoulder pads that include a spine protector.

Gloves ▶

Your gloves should meet or slightly overlap your elbow pads. They should have hard protection on the back of the hand and a flexible palm. Your fingertips shouldn't be touching the end of your glove — they could get hurt by sticks if they do.

Shin pads ▶

Be sure there is a gap between your shin and the outside hard padding of your shin pad. Instead of your shin, that gap will take the force of a hit. Your kneecap should sit in the kneecap pad, while the bottom of your shin pad reaches to your skate laces without making it difficult for you to skate.

◀ Neck guard

You must wear one in Canada but you don't have to in the United States. A neck guard protects you from cuts by skates or sticks. It should fit comfortably around your neck.

◀ Elbow pads

Look for elbow pads with solid-plastic elbow caps and forearm protection. Make sure they are snug so they won't twist or fall out of place.

◀ Pants

Your pant legs should stop just above your kneecaps, and the hip pads should fit over your hips. Look for pants with good padding over your tailbone, hips and the front of your thighs.

▶ Helmet and face mask

Look for a sticker on the helmet and face shield that says they meet government safety standards. Make sure the chin cup fits snugly on your chin and the top of the mask rests inside the J-clips on the side of the helmet. This will prevent your mask from jamming into your mouth.

If you wear a plastic visor, you'll need to use a cleaner and defogger at times so that you can see well. If you don't want to bother with this or the scratches that may force you to replace the visor often, try wearing a wire mask.

◀ Mouth guard

This is required equipment in the United States but not in Canada. Wearing a mouth guard helps prevent jaw injuries and concussions. Mouth guards without straps must be colored, so if they fall out on the ice, they're easy to find.

Jill

This protects your pelvic area. It should fit snugly but not hinder your skating.

Garter belt

Use this to keep your socks from falling down, or choose a pair of hockey shorts that have Velcro to hold up your socks and a pouch for your jill.

Some hockey equipment is being specially designed for girls. Check it out with the rest of the gear to see what fits you best. Find out about hockey sticks on page 16.

 EXPERT TIP

To make sure your equipment fits right, try on new equipment with the equipment that goes next to it. For example, wear your gloves and shoulder pads when you are trying on elbow pads to see how they all fit together.

See how there's no gap between this player's gloves, elbow pads and shoulder pads? That means they fit her well.

Gear for Goalies

As a goalie you have to get in front of a hard rubber puck that's being fired at you from all directions. Make sure you're dressed for it.

Mask ▶

Whether you wear a helmet-mask combination or a fitted face-mask, look for the sticker that says it's safety approved. A fiberglass mask is the only one that can be painted and only with fiberglass paint.

Neck guard ▶

In Canada you must wear a neck guard. In some areas you must also attach a plastic neck guard to your mask to deflect sticks and pucks.

◄ Chest protector

Look for a protector that has wings to protect your shoulders and extra protection on the inner upper arm of the glove hand and on the outer upper arm of the blocker hand. These pieces can be added to a protector that you have.

◄ Glove and blocker

Look for a junior size; you probably don't need a senior size until you're over 13. Can you handle your stick with the blocker you choose?

◄ Goalie pads

Get pads that overlap your pants by about 12.5 cm (5 in.). The middle knee-rib should be at the center of your knee. Knee cups protect you when you drop to your knees. These come as part of some pads, or you may add them to yours. You may also add a thigh protector, so when you're on your knees the space between your pants and pads is covered.

Goalie jill

You wear a jill similar to those worn by your teammates, except that yours has more protection. Be sure to wear one!

Goalie pants

These have extra padding in the inner thigh, tailbone and front hip areas.

Goalie skates

Goalie skates have hard plastic on the toe, heel and sides for added protection against pucks and sticks. Your goalie skates fit the same way regular skates do (see page 14). The radius of the blade is usually 26 ft. or 28 ft., which is nearly flat (see page 14). This helps you stay balanced.

Goalie stick

Choose junior, intermediate or senior size. Sticks also come in various lies, from 13 to 18. The lie is the angle between the heel of the blade and the shaft. Most players ages 8 to 12 use a lie of 13 or 14. Be sure to use the lie that allows you to keep the blade of your stick flat on the ice when you're in your goalie stance (see page 26). As you grow taller, the lie will increase. Try different lies as you develop your goaltending style.

To ensure your stick is the right length, get into your goalie stance. When you hold the stick just above the paddle, with the blade flat on the ice, your hand should be about knee level. A goalie stick is balanced when it's made, so don't cut it.

(see page 14)

No matter what position you play, air your equipment after each time you use it to prevent rashes and bad smells. Once in a while, wash any equipment that lies next to your skin (except your gloves) in a washing machine and lay it out to dry.

 ★ PROFILE ★

Manon Rhéaume
Canada, 1992, 1994, 1998

Manon Rhéaume is a two-time World Champion and Olympic silver medalist for Team Canada. When she played an exhibition game before the 1992 season with the Tampa Bay Lightning, she also became the first woman to play in the National Hockey League. "Believe in yourself," says Rhéaume, "and focus only on what you can control."

Skate Smarts

Skates are your most important hockey equipment. Getting ones that fit right is key, but that isn't always easy. Usually you grow quickly between the ages of 8 and 12. It can become expensive if you always buy skates that fit your feet perfectly, because they leave you no room to grow.

To get the best fit, have your feet measured when you buy your skates. If that isn't possible, take the insoles out of the skates, and stand on the insoles with your heels at the very backs. You should have about 1.25 cm (½ in.), no more, of space in front of your longest toe. This will give you about a size to grow into. Don't buy your skates any bigger than that.

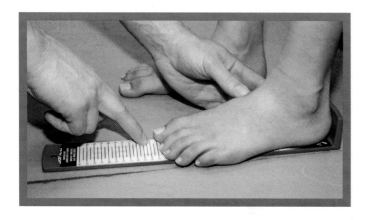

Be sure the skate's arch is in the same place as yours. When your growing slows down or stops, fit your skates so your toes just touch the end of the boots or, when you stand on the insoles, you don't have any room in front of your big toes.

Get the edge

Before you buy your skates, check that each blade is straight and flat with no large nicks. Most skates for 8- to 12-year-olds have a 9-foot radius (also called profile or rocker). The radius is the curve of the bottom of the skate blade from front to back.

As the number of the radius goes up, so does the part of the blade that touches the ice when the blade is flat on the ice. Have you ever watched speed skaters? Their skates have a much larger radius than hockey players' skates do. That allows them to go very fast, but they can't turn sharply. In skates with a smaller radius, you may skate a little slower, but you'll turn faster.

Stay sharp

When you take your skates to get sharpened for the first time, ask for a 9-foot radius. If you're a beginner, you may want to ask for a sharpening that will tilt you forward a little. This helps to keep you from falling over backward and forces you to bend your knees.

Some experienced players use heel lifts to force them to bend their knees more and lean forward so they can skate faster. As you grow you may want to experiment with this and try an 11-foot radius for more speed.

Dry your blades with a cloth after each use and use skate guards to protect them. To dry your skates, take out the insoles and turn the skates upside down. Don't dry them on heaters, because that dries out the glues and makes your skates stiff.

→ **Try It!**

I hate buying new skates because I don't like breaking them in. Do you feel the same way? To soften new skates, try pulling them on over warm, wet socks, then wear your skates (and skate guards) around your home for about 30 minutes.

You can also ask your local sports store if it has a skate oven. After your skates are heated in the oven, you wear them for a short time while they mold to your feet.

Stick with It

Don't you love getting a new hockey stick? I do, but deciding on the right one is difficult. Here are a few facts to help you choose.

Sticks were first made of wood, but now they're also made of aluminum, graphite and Kevlar. You can put together some sticks yourself, using a separate shaft (the long, upright part) and blade (the part you use to direct the puck). Certain blades attach with keys.

◀ **The key lets you add or remove certain blades from shafts.**

▶ **The heat gun expands the shaft and softens the glue on the blade.**

You attach other shafts and blades by heating the shaft and the glue on the blade, and then sliding the blade into the shaft. This requires a heater, such as a heat gun, and some strength to get the blade in or out of the shaft. If you buy a stick like this, get an adult to change the blade or help you do it.

To get power in your shot, you need to be able to bend the shaft of your stick a little when you push down on it. The amount the shaft bends is called its flex. Junior sticks are the most flexible and have small grips so you can handle them easily. They're recommended for most players ages 8 to 12. As you get taller and stronger you'll want an intermediate or senior stick. Before I buy a different stick, I ask to try out my teammates' sticks to see which ones I like best.

Blades come in many different curves, which are called patterns. These can help you handle the puck and raise it off the ice on your forehand. However, the greater the curve, the more difficult it is for you to lift backhand shots.

▲ Here are four blade patterns.

When you buy a stick, chances are that you will need to cut it to fit you. Stand in your skates with the stick standing straight in front of you. The butt end of the stick should reach somewhere between your chest and your chin. If you know you'll have to cut your stick, buy one with a little more flex, because your stick will get stiffer when you cut it.

Be sure your stick is the right lie (see page 13) for you. One way to do this is to check that the tape on the bottom of your stick is wearing evenly. If it wears more on the toe of your stick, decrease the lie of your stick. Increase the lie if it wears more on the heel. Popular players' names are now stamped on sticks to indicate lies and blade patterns.

Taping tips

● Use white tape on the butt of your stick (colored tape has chemicals in it that destroy the palms of your gloves).

● Tape the blade of your stick from heel to toe.

● Make sure the blade is dry so the tape sticks better. You may also wax the tape on your blade to help prevent snow from sticking to it.

● Keep the tape pulled tight as you wrap it around your stick so you won't get wrinkles in your taping.

As you continue to play you'll learn the type of stick, length, curve and taping that works best for you. You may also try "doctoring" your stick to make it fit your needs even better. Some experienced players heat up the blade and curve it exactly the way they like it.

Always remember though, it's *you* who controls your stick. When you make a great pass, *you* did it, and when you make a not-so-great pass, *you* did that, too — *not your stick*.

Off-Ice Training

I often wish I had my own hockey rink so I could play any time. How about you? Even though you may not be able to get as much ice time as you want, you can do many things to be your best when you step on the ice. Increase your fitness and strength by playing other sports and by participating in physical activities all year round. Here are some other ideas.

Get flexible

Flexibility is key to getting the most out of your muscles and preventing injuries such as muscle strains. Be sure to follow these tips:

● Before practices and games, warm up your muscles with some light movement (such as jogging, jumping jacks, dancing) until you're just starting to sweat.

● Slowly go into each stretch, hold for 15 to 20 seconds and don't bounce.

● Repeat the stretch three times.

● Be sure to stretch both sides of your body.

Hamstrings stretch

Sit as shown in the photo. Bend from the waist, keeping your head up and your back straight, until you feel a slight stretch in the back of your upper leg.

Here are just a few of the stretches that help loosen up your skating muscles.

Groin stretch

Sit as shown. Slowly bring your feet close to your body until you feel a light stretch in your groin area. Use your elbows to press down lightly on your knees if you need more of a stretch.

Quadriceps stretch

Stand as shown, making sure your knees are touching. Bring your heel to your buttocks. You should feel a stretch in the front of your bent leg. If you are having trouble balancing, place one finger of your free hand on your belly button.

→ Try It!

Turn your team's dressing room into a warmup room. First, clear the floor by placing all the equipment bags on the benches. Check that everyone has warmup shoes and clothes, and a mat or towel. Play music that the whole team likes.

Follow the stretching tips and let each player lead an exercise. Make the warmup part of your pre-game routine. It warms up your body and gets your mind ready to play, too. Cool down after each game with light movement and stretching.

Jump to the beat!

Hip flexors stretch

Kneel as shown in the picture. Without bending at the waist, push your hips forward to feel a stretch in the front of your hip.

Sensational Skating

Skating is the most important of all skills in hockey. Here are a few tips to help you become a better skater.

▼ Starting

The V-start is the quickest way to get moving. Place your feet shoulder-width apart, point your toes outward, lean forward and bend your hips, knees and ankles to a 45-degree angle. Extend your hip, knee and then your ankle with all your strength. Make your first three or four strides as quickly as you can.

▲ Stopping

The two-foot stop is the one most players use. You turn quickly, bend your legs and dig your edges into the ice. If you stop with your right side forward, you use the inside edge of your right skate and the outside edge of your left. Reverse this to stop with your left side forward. Most players have more difficulty stopping on one side than the other. Try stopping on your weaker side during practice drills.

▶ Do it backward

Defense players often have to skate backward as they face their opponents, but every player needs to develop this skill. Take the position in the photo. Alternating feet, move backward using your skates to make Cs in the ice. Bring each skate back underneath your body beside the other before you begin your next C-cut.

If you find yourself falling forward, try sitting down as if you're in a chair. Whether you are practicing forward or backward skating, this is a great way to develop proper technique and strengthen your legs.

▼ Have fun getting better

Play frozen tag to practice skating. This improves your anaerobic fitness (that's your ability to work hard for a short time). Improve your balance and agility by jumping over lines on both feet and then one foot. Try turning 180 degrees and 360 degrees in the air. See how fast you can go down on your stomach, roll over and get up.

→ Try It!

- Get extra skating practice during public skating time.

- Hit the ice early for practice so you can use any free time before practice starts.

- Focus on skills that you need to improve. This takes discipline, as it's a lot more fun to do the things you're already good at.

★ PROFILE ★

Alana Blahoski
USA, 1996–present

Forward Alana Blahoski is one of the fastest skaters in women's hockey. She knows how to use her speed to pressure opponents into making mistakes. Blahoski's excellent skating skills also make her a top penalty-killer. Her talent for playing on the shorthand helped Team USA win Olympic gold in 1998.

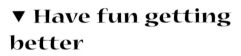

Shoot to Score ⋯⋯⋯⋯⋯⋯⋯ ●

Scoring on a top goalie is one of the greatest feelings in the world. Improve your chances of scoring by perfecting a variety of shots.

The wrist shot is one of the most deceptive shots because the goalie can't tell when the puck is going to leave your stick. Since it doesn't have a big wind-up, this is a great shot to use when you're in heavy traffic and need to shoot quickly.

▼ As you release the puck, quickly pull the stick back with your top hand and push it forward with your bottom hand.

▼ At the end of your follow-through, make sure the curved side of your blade is facing the ice and your stick is pointing at your target.

▲ To take a wrist shot, move your stick along the ice in a sweeping motion with the puck spinning from the heel of your blade to the tip.

When you're driving to the net or battling for a rebound, you often don't have time to change position and take a forehand shot. Surprise the goaltender and unleash your backhand. A backhand shot is tricky for a goalie because she usually doesn't expect it. It's like a wrist shot, except the puck comes off the back of your blade.

The slapshot is the most powerful shot because of its big wind-up. For this shot, lower your bottom hand on the stick as you bring the stick back off the ice to about shoulder height. As you bring your stick down, the middle of the blade to the toe contacts the ice before it strikes the puck. Follow through as you do for a wrist shot.

► Cassie Campbell points her stick at the target as she follows through on a slapshot.

All players use slapshots, usually when they have time and are shooting from far away. Defense players use them most because they often shoot from just inside the opponent's blue line. These are known as point shots. You should keep your point shot low so there is more chance of a rebound and less chance of injury to one of your forwards who is screening in front of the net.

For a flip shot, you use the tip of your blade to quickly scoop the puck high in the air. You can do this on your forehand and backhand. Use a flip shot to flick the puck over a sprawling goalie when you are in tight to the net, or use it to clear the puck out of your end.

→ **Try It!**

To be a real hot shot, be sure to practice — even when you're not on the ice. A sheet of hard plastic such as a Crazy Carpet (or plastic toboggan) placed on a solid surface makes a great shooting surface because the puck will slide on it. It should be at least 1.2 m (4 ft.) long and 30 cm (1 ft.) wide.

Lay your plastic flat in front of your target. A ball-field backstop or a cement wall makes a good target, but get permission to use it since the puck may leave marks.

Now start practicing:

• Aim for targets, or visualize a goalie and shoot for the openings.

• Vary your stance (sideways, face on, on one foot) and distance from the goal.

• Practice releasing the puck quickly using forehand and backhand shots.

• Scatter a number of pucks on your plastic. Pretend you are shooting a rebound and use your flip shot to scoop the pucks up quickly, one after the other.

Get in the Passing Lane

You receive a breakout pass but suddenly one of the other team's defense players is in your face. So you bank the puck off the boards to your center and jump around the defense to join the rush. As you drive to the net, your center gives you a perfect pass. You shoot. You score — all thanks to the practice your line has put into passing.

Pass the puck

You'll make a better pass if you

● Call your teammate's name or catch her eye before passing the puck to her.

● Push the puck off your blade, don't slap it.

● Visualize shooting the puck from the tape on your stick blade right onto the tape on your teammate's blade.

● Bank the puck off the boards to help you pass the puck by an opponent.

● Aim your pass to where your teammate will be when the puck arrives.

Be ready to receive a pass

● Call for the pass. Shout "Up," "Boards," "Over" or "Back" to your teammate so she knows where you want the pass.

● Put your stick on the ice to give your teammate a target.

● Position yourself so nobody is between you and your teammate.

● Cushion the puck when it hits your stick. That way it won't bounce off.

● Practice receiving a pass on your forehand, backhand and in your skates.

Puckhandling

Here are a few simple things you can do to improve your puckhandling. To carry the puck past an opponent, fake one direction with your head, shoulder or stick, and then go the other way. Try approaching your opponent at less than full speed, so you can burst by her after you fake. To stop her from knocking the puck off your stick, keep your body between her and the puck (this is called puck protection) as you speed by and cut to the net.

→ **Try It!**

Place two pucks 60 to 100 cm (2 to 3 ft.) apart. Use the toe of your stick to move a third puck in a figure 8 around them. Treat the puck as if it will break when slapped too hard, and try to keep your upper body, wrists and hands loose.

Danielle Goyette
Canada, 1992

Danielle Goyette has led Team Canada in scoring at many competitions including the 1998 Olympics. She handles the puck as if it's glued to her stick — Goyette has the scoring "touch."

Goyette developed her skills as a young girl on an outdoor rink repeating goals she'd seen in National Hockey League games on television. You may not have a rink close by, but you can practice with a ball or roller-hockey puck.

Goaltending Skills

"Time! Time!" you shout from your goal to one of your defense. Now she knows that she can get the puck in the corner and take time to look for the right play to make.

Communicating on the ice is just one of the skills goaltenders need to have. Here are a few more.

Take your stance

Get into your goalie stance in front of a mirror, look at this photo, then compare to see if you have the correct position. Make sure your stick is flat on the ice, 10 to 15 cm (4 to 6 in.) in front of your skates, so you can cushion the rebound on low shots.

Hold your glove and blocker in front of you so you can watch the puck all the way into them as you're making the save. Make sure they don't cover an area that's already covered by another part of your body. Keep your glove open at knee height; it's easier to move it up than down. When you move on the ice, be sure not to lift up out of your stance, and keep your weight on the balls of your feet.

Playing the angles

Ever watched a goaltender who always seems to be where the puck is shot, but without moving a lot? She's actually adjusting her position constantly. When the puck is shot, she's in the best possible position to make the save.

Being able to quickly move forward, backward and from side to side on your skates is a must for proper positioning. Practice staying in your stance while moving around your crease. Imagine that the puck has eyes: your mission is to always be in position so the puck "sees" as little net as possible.

When the puck is above the hash marks (the lines on each side of the face-off circle), imagine a line drawn from the puck to the midpoint of the goal line. Take your stance with one foot on either side of the line. Challenge the shooter by moving out of your net toward the puck. This decreases the amount of open net the puck can hit.

When you challenge, be sure to stay in your compact stance with a good knee bend, and point both shoulders at the puck to stay "square" to it.

If the shooter is coming from a sharp angle (for example, from between the face-off dot to the goal line), position yourself next to the goalpost closest to the player to force her to shoot across your body to the far side. That way you will only have to move in one direction.

→ Try It!

Here's an off-ice drill to improve your concentration and coordination. Wearing your glove, blocker and mask, get into your goalie stance facing a wall 4.6 m (15 ft.) away. Have someone stand behind you and throw a tennis ball at the wall. Vary your distance from the wall, the speed of the throw and the time in between saves.

Goalies have to be very flexible. The exercises on page 18 will help.

Tips from an Olympic Coach

Coaches are your teachers when it comes to learning hockey skills. How much you improve, however, depends on how hard you are willing to work. How much talent you have is not as important as what you do with it.

Shannon Miller knows that. She is one of the top hockey coaches in the world, with a record of 15 wins and zero losses in World Championship play on her way to three gold medals. Miller was the only female head coach at the 1998 Olympics, where she led Team Canada to a silver medal.

Miller coached the team to Pacific Rim gold medals in 1995 and 1996 and to a fourth straight World Championship gold medal in 1997. Miller is now head coach at the University of Minnesota Duluth (UMD). Find out how she chooses her players.

Q: **Shannon, what do you look for in a player?**

A: There are three things that I look at. One is talent in a specific area. Is this player a great checker, playmaker or goal scorer?

Just as important, though, is her character. A player who is unselfish, respectful and understands the importance of "team" is invaluable. If she has the courage to do the best she can and keep on trying, then she's the type of player I want on my team.

I also look for an athlete who brings intensity and competitiveness to each task, whether it be a game or doing bike sprints.

► Lori Dupuis takes direction from Coach Miller between shifts during the final of the 1997 World Championships.

Q: **What advice would you give to a young hockey player?**

A: To enjoy herself all the time she's on the ice. She should share that with her teammates and really cherish those friendships she develops through hockey.

Q: **What about trying to make it on a high-performance team, such as a national team?**

A: First a player needs to recognize what she's good at. For example, is she a natural goal scorer or more of a defensive forward? Then she needs to focus on her strengths, putting her energy into becoming the best she can be in that role.

Q: **Do you have any other messages for a girl who wants to excel?**

A: To become her best she must set goals and approach each training session and game with a purpose. It is important to balance on-ice training, off-ice training, and rest and recovery periods. Recovery time is as important as training time and is essential to performing at your best consistently.

I recommend a player have a dream goal, setting other goals along the way and enjoying the challenge.

▲ Coach Miller calls out the next line during a UMD game.

Maria Rooth
Sweden, 1995–present

Maria Rooth works hard and is committed to being the best she can be in all areas of her game. That's why Shannon Miller recruited this forward to play at UMD. Rooth brings goal-scoring talent and experience to Miller's team; she played for Team Sweden at the 1998 Olympics and was one of Sweden's top three players at the 1997 World Championships.

Rooth appreciates working with Coach Miller, as well as UMD's two assistant coaches. "Having coaches who have a variety of strengths is great," says Rooth. "They help me improve all parts of my game — on-ice skills, physical fitness and mental toughness."

Team Play — Be Part of It

Your team is going into overtime. You huddle with your line and talk about how you really need to work together to get the job done.

"Everyone take a deep breath," says your coach. "Concentrate only on what you need to do during your shift." She knows that if you focus on the outcome of a game, you will get nervous. You won't focus on your shift, and so you may not perform your best. After the coach's pep talk, a teammate yells, "We can do it!"

Whether you win or lose a game, it is a total team effort. Being part of a team is a privilege and a special experience. Each player contributes something unique. Are you the player who keeps everyone loose? Do you score a lot of goals? Or do you make things happen each shift? On Team Canada, a few of my roles were to be a leader, kill penalties and play solid defensive hockey.

You probably are a combination of a few roles at different times too, but whatever part you play, you are important to the success of your team. So take pride in your role and do it the best you can. Also make sure you let your teammates know that you appreciate the roles they play on the team.

◄ One of the things I emphasize at my hockey school is that practice is the time to try new plays. It's okay to make mistakes. You won't do everything right the first time, but if you don't push yourself, you won't learn.

Here are what some of the top players in the world think "team" means.

Jennifer Botterill
Canada, 1998–present

The youngest member of Team Canada at the 1998 Olympics, Jennifer Botterill plays forward. She's as good at defending as she is at scoring goals. Botterill says, "If you're a team player, you're willing to put others ahead of yourself. You always do what's best for the team, and you're not at all focused or concerned with individual results."

Lisa Brown Miller
USA, 1990–1998

Lisa Brown Miller exemplified the meaning of team player from 1990 to 1998 playing forward for Team USA. On every shift she played, she made good things happen for her team. Brown Miller focused her energy and determination on making plays, not just on scoring goals. She was also known for pressuring opponents into making mistakes. "A team player should take each shift as a chance to do her best in her role, for the benefit of the team," says Brown Miller.

→ Try It!

The next time your team faces what appears to be a negative situation, play the "No-Negatives" game with your teammates. For 30 seconds rattle off as many good things about the situation as possible. Remember, no negatives allowed!

I played the No-Negatives game when I dislocated my shoulder during the first practice of the Three Nations Cup in 1996. I was disappointed and in a lot of pain, but I said to myself, "Now I'll get a chance to learn from watching. I can also make my shoulder really strong before the World Championships. Maybe I can do color commentary with the cable TV station covering the Three Nations Cup. And I can sleep in tomorrow and have my teammates wait on me for a day!"

Game Day

Do you look forward to playing every hockey game? Players on national teams are no different. Every game day was a special time, and we used the whole day to prepare for the competition that night. Here's how.

8:15 A.M. The team gets together for a healthy breakfast. We usually have a lot of choice, everything from eggs to pancakes. I like juice, bagels and cereal.

9:00 A.M. We discuss tonight's game as we bus from our hotel to the arena.

9:15 A.M. I tape my stick, chat and warm up for practice. I have a badly bruised ankle, so I get our physiotherapist to put a pad on it. On the outside of my skate I'll also wear a special protector that our equipment manager designed.

10:15 A.M. On the ice. Since it's game day, we don't have a full practice. Instead we skate, pass and take shots at the goalies for about 40 minutes to stay sharp.

11:00–11:45 A.M. I cool down, shower and head for the bus back to the hotel.

12:15 P.M. After that practice I'm ready for lunch. I like a salad, chicken, rice and fruit. And there are chocolate chip cookies, one of the team's favorites—and mine!

1:00 P.M. Naptime. Before I fall asleep for a couple of hours, I visualize the new breakout system we're trying in tonight's game.

3:45 P.M. I join the team for our pre-game meal, which is usually pasta, potatoes or rice with fish or chicken. I grab a banana and granola bar in case I get hungry before the game. I also drink lots of water throughout the day.

4:30 P.M. A team walk gives us a chance to get some fresh air, move and relax.

5:00 P.M. Our coach goes over the game plan and meets with forward lines, defense pairs and goalies. It helps to watch videos of our team and our opponents. I meet with my wingers to talk over our line's strategy for tonight's game.

6:00 P.M. On the way back to the arena we joke and sing our team song.

6:15 P.M. We check our sticks and skates, and get any injuries looked over again. I visualize being energized and strong.

6:40 P.M. For 15 minutes we work up a sweat and stretch to music. We end our off-ice warmup the same way each time, with a cheer and some hand-slapping.

7:25 P.M. We're on the ice for 20 minutes. Shooting, skating and passing help loosen us up.

7:45 P.M. Time to relax in the dressing room while the ice is resurfaced. Our coach comes in for a few minutes to remind us of the game plan and to pump us up.

8:00 P.M. The starting lineups are announced and the game begins. Our team plays great and we win 4–1! The new breakout worked just the way it did in practice. My line didn't get scored against, and I scored once and got an assist.

10:30 P.M. I cool down, shower and do a couple of interviews with reporters.

11:15 P.M. We sign autographs on our way out to the bus. It's great to meet fans.

11:45 P.M. We dig in and enjoy a big post-game meal — more pasta and chicken for me. Then it's off to bed so we'll be rested for tomorrow's game.

Hockey Star Up Close

Karyn Bye has played for Team USA since 1992 and was assistant captain at the 1998 Olympics. With her powerful shot, Bye's a dominant player on the ice. Take a look at how she got there.

▼ Not only was Bye the only girl on her team, but she was also captain.

Q: **When did you get started playing hockey?**

A: I started playing when I was seven. My older brother Chris was sick and couldn't go to practice, so I put on his equipment and tried to fool the guys on his team. After a while they figured out I wasn't him, but I kept playing. I was the only girl on the River Falls Youth Hockey team in River Falls, Wisconsin.

Q: **Was it tough being the only girl?**

A: For the most part the guys on my team accepted me as "one of the guys." But sometimes a player from the other team would take a cheap shot at me. I think I crushed a few male egos when I scored goals on those guys!

If anything ever happened to me, it was as if I had 19 brothers out there to protect me. The only other obstacle I can think of was always having to change in the bathroom — I hated having to do that!

◀ Bye's team placed first at a tournament in 1980.

▶ Here's Bye in her first year of playing hockey.

Q: **When did going to the Olympics become your dream?**

A: When I was eight years old, I watched the 1980 American Men's Olympic Team bring home the gold. It was at that time I said, "I want to go to the Olympics." My dream finally came true 18 years later!

Q: **What did you do to make your dream come true?**

A: Each year I would set new goals for myself. For example, when I was 14, I wanted to make the boys' high-school team. After I made the team in the tenth grade, my goal was to receive an athletic scholarship to play women's college hockey, which I did at the University of New Hampshire.

Q: **What advice would you give to girls who play hockey?**

A: Work hard, set goals and, most important, have fun! The more ice time you get, the better you will become. To achieve your goals you have to be dedicated, be ready to make sacrifices and commit yourself to what you want to do.

Q: **What have you learned from pursuing your dream?**

A: I've learned that in order to be the best, you have to dedicate yourself to what you are doing and give 110 percent at all times. You can learn a lot when playing on a team with 19 other people all working toward the same goal.

Q: **What are your goals for the future?**

A: To keep playing hockey as long as I'm having fun and making the team. I also want to try broadcasting, coaching and maybe working for a National Hockey League team.

▲ Bye was Team USA's top scorer at the 1998 Winter Olympics.

▼ Winning Olympic Gold was a dream Bye worked hard to make come true.

Player Profiles

Meet more of the incredible women's hockey players from all over the world.

▼ Tara Mounsey

USA, 1997–present

Tara Mounsey is one of the best defense players in the world. She has superior skating skills and a booming shot that she has used to score game-winning goals. Mounsey led her team's defense in scoring at the 1998 Olympics; she earned six points as the U.S. went on to capture the gold medal. She also won a World Championship silver medal in 1997 and 1999.

▼ Riikka Nieminen

Finland, 1990–present

First in Olympic scoring in 1998 with 12 points, this top forward led Finland to a bronze medal. Riika Nieminen is lightning fast and handles the puck as if it's stuck to her stick. She was named to the all-star team at the 1992, 1994 and 1997 Worlds and named best forward in 1994.

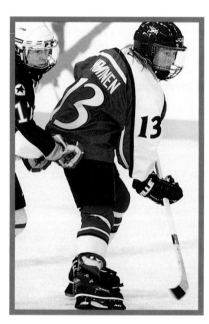

▼ Hayley Wickenheiser

Canada, 1994–present

At age 15, Hayley Wickenheiser won her first World Championship gold medal with Team Canada. Her power, size and speed make her a dominant force whenever she steps on the ice. She has one of the hardest and quickest released shots in women's hockey and is a threat to score from almost anywhere.

▼ Jayna Hefford

Canada, 1997–present

This speedy forward has earned two World Championship gold medals and an Olympic silver medal since she joined Team Canada. Jayna Hefford possesses a great burst of speed that she cleverly uses to get around defense players, and she has great hands to put the puck in the net. She was second on Team Canada in scoring through the 1997–98 exhibition season, with 19 goals and 5 assists in 21 games.

▼ Sarah Tueting

USA, 1998–present

Goalie Sarah Tueting carefully plans and prepares for every game. For example, she has a habit of always putting on her right skate before her left one. Tueting is a fast-moving goaltender with quick reflexes. At age 21, she used her butterfly style with confidence to stop 21 of 22 shots in the Olympic gold-medal game.

What's Next for Women's Hockey?

You may see a professional hockey league for women in the future. Women's hockey is growing and changing so quickly that organizations in the United States and Canada have started talking about the possibility. I can't wait to attend a game!

You'll also get the chance to see your country's women's hockey team play more often. World Championships have been held in 1990, 1992, 1994, 1997 and 1999, with the top eight teams in the world competing. Now they'll face off against each other in the World Championships every year.

Teams from Denmark, Finland, Germany, Norway, Russia, Sweden, Switzerland and other countries compete in the European Championships each year. The top five teams from this tournament go on to compete at the World Championships.

Canada, Finland and the United States have competed for the Three Nations Cup each year since 1996, and the Pacific Rim Championships hosted Canada, China, Japan and the U.S. in 1995 and 1996. Look for more tournaments and exhibition games between countries in the future. Now, of course, you can watch countries compete for Olympic gold every four years.

There are more opportunities for women to play hockey than ever before. In the U.S. there are many women's college teams, with more starting every year. Some offer scholarships to players from all over the world. Many Canadian universities are also adding women's hockey to their programs.

Junior national teams have played in some international competitions, and you'll likely see more. Also look for more national competitions for girls under the age of 18 in Canada and the U.S. So lace up your skates, grab your stick and enjoy all the exciting opportunities women's hockey can offer.

▲ I've been training girls at my hockey camp since 1995.